MW01324184

the Sutler

Also by Michael Kenyon

Fiction

Kleinberg (Oolichan Books)
Pinocchio's Wife (Oberon)
Durable Tumblers (Oolichan Books)

Poetry

Rack of Lamb (Brick Books) (prose poems)

the Sutler

Michael Kenyon

Brick Books

Library and Archives Canada Cataloguing in Publication

Kenyon, Michael, 1953 –
The Sutler / Michael Kenyon.

Poems.
ISBN 1-894078-41-1

I. Title.

PS8571.E572S88 2005 C811'.54 C2005-900401-0

We acknowledge the support of the Canada Council for the Arts, the Government of Canada through the Book Publishing Industry Development Program (BPIDP), and the Ontario Arts Council for their support of our publishing program.

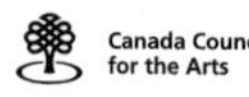

Conseil des Arts
du Canada

Canada

The cover painting is by Lorraine Thomson, "Below Night," acrylic on paper, 11.5" x 15.25", 1997.

The author's photograph is by Lorraine Thomson.

The book is set in Novarese, Officina and AlOz Brush.

Design and layout by Alan Siu.

Printed by Sunville Printco Inc.

Brick Books
431 Boler Road, Box 20081
London, Ontario N6K 4G6

www.brickbooks.ca

30 Years Young
Brick Books 1975–2005

This book is for Lorraine

Contents

The ice age

After the duel 11
Angels 13
Another Sistine Chapel 14
Cabin 15
Cayuga 16
Control, power, secrecy 17
Fitful 18
General conditions 19
Goodbye 20
Heart room 21
Hope Bay 22
In the living room in summer 24
New Year 25
Now that we are 26
Shortcut 27
Songs the voice heard 28
This longing 29
Twin beds in the Bath Y 30
When she told me 32
Love has eaten us 33
Ferry 34
After the ice age 35

Battlefield

Death of a samurai 41
- Agony 43
- Samurai 44
- Vancouver from England 45
- I love Mifune 46
- Apprentice 47
- Last battle 48

Last words 50
The noise of their industry 51
Grace 52
Lesson 53
Well/Spring 54
The Sutler 55

The rising body

The rising body 67
After the divorce 68
Flash in the pan 69
Before night 70
Balloonists 71
Prison life 72
These seeds, a full jar 73
At the rubbish heap 74
Behind the community centre 75
I believed in things 76
Cousin 77
Crescent Beach 78
Dry August 79
Friday before work 80
Living alone 81
Talisman 84
After Seattle 85
The sisters and the goat 86
Undersea Gardens 87
Keeping watch 88

Acknowledgments 91
About the author 93

The ice age

After the duel

I killed her, yes, and now the sun is bright. No
sign of yesterday's crime. Scarcely
any beach, and that metre-deep in slick weed
whose surface is a carpet of flies
that rises with each sloppy step. So
this is what tomorrow is like.

We arrived in enough daylight to unpack
the Scotch and mark a path between the bed
and the table to the hot tub on the deck,
then we set aside our watches and
I split kindling and lit the fire while
she cut up potatoes and boiled water.

A short November day and heavy. Sun
a wide laser on the waves, the water fat,
brimming, the bay's arms angled
not quite right, nothing to hold
properly what I committed in passion's
name. Everything bulging with what's hid.

A drink in the hot tub, another by the fire.
Every time we reached the point of saying
what we wanted we took hits from the bottle
or slipped under the rain and steam. We were
choosing weapons. I honed sex, she polished
the difference between life and death.

Down at the boat house at Point-No-Point
the last wind faint in the sunny cove. Sunny?
Blasted by sun, the surf white and the beach
knee-deep in foam from the night that roared so
two sets of inland tourists checked out
before dawn, terrified of the storm.

The place of the duel is always desolate:
food, whisky, talk, all done. The dance
is an old one, steps well rehearsed, though
the first cut's a surprise. I play dead while
she wails and beats the air with her fists.
I'm a carapace, empty and upturned, and

her fury makes her careless. Along
the road in pitch black night I listen
to the trees hiss. The cabin's too small
when I return, so full of smoke that
it's not clear at first that we're finished.
All night the walls shook and the surf

boomed. Love, I'm losing it. A glossy crow
picks through the wrack, unfolds in sunshine. Soon
will be solstice and I'll break. She joins me
at the boat house and we choose stones for a game
of boules; she knocks me out of the circle
every time. No one answers. No one hears.

Angels

They come in off the mud, their torn wings
half-hidden by Mackinaws, and plunge into
the forest as if into an element heavier than the salt-
chuck that crashes behind them. They wade close to

where we hide. Why is it so hard to speak
of what we love? This is the storm we've been
telling stories about. These angels
know the island we've chosen: lonely yet

sheltered by other islands, no beach open
to open sea. That's why they arrange boats to carry us
beyond a biology that will break anything: their mouths wide
in the squall. How let them know we can't hear ourselves?

Nothing to be done.
Waiting is full of loss, but what else is waiting for?
When the moment comes
the wind twangs like laundry long ago,

something of childhood that snaps but doesn't hurt.
We won't look at each other. Gently
they unlace our fingers and separate us and in a blink
we're far apart, a long way from home, in separate boats

already sailing. I look for the light to port
but already she's
turned away, small,
smaller.

Another Sistine Chapel

On the phone to a lost wife I try this: How far away
do you have to go for me to want you? She says,
You don't understand the limits of the body.

If I want you, I say, you are perfect. If you aren't,
I want candles, soap, and salt. Listen to her thinking.
Desire creates perfection? she says. We hang up
and still I don't know I'm sad. I walk the dog.

I want something because it's perfect, the wanting
produces perfection. The gestures of desire are
claiming (in relation to), possessing (outside the
body), consuming (inside the body). And

when the geese stop crossing overhead and
horizons stay put and my dog has grown
patient with age, I will remember this road.
She painted the ceiling, had the dream.

I know this. Now what is my dream?
My dog is looking at me. I've come
to a standstill. One leaf falls and I'm rocked
back to every leaf-

twirling squall along every tree-
lined street long ago. Next please. Dying,
I remember this and how much I loved her.

Cabin

Too long in the hot tub. Too long on the top rail,
ankles hooked round the uprights, looking
straight out to Japan while rain pricks bare
shoulders and my wife prowls inside. This
is not my game but I paid for the chips.
Begging the question.

I'm lightheaded while she weeps and punches the air
and asks for breath, for the Pacific to invade Juan
de Fuca and change her mind. Then she licks
a pencil and makes notes while I shudder
giving birth to some emptiness I thought
was long gone. Call these small thoughts,

I dare you: at Point-No-Point I remember
when our cat disappeared. We found her in the hedge
that spring. Can you tell when your life
is over? Can you know what you know?
This is shit, this. I can't recognize
even a tree. I imagine this horror is about sex

when it's clear that it's geology. I wear
a terry bathrobe. She puts on a shirt and jeans. Pick
a number, make a bet–it's tectonics, entirely, syncopation
of the plates. We're down to earth, to a fault, and what
we do when left to our own
devices.

Cayuga

Before she started to stink the males jumped her
with greater regularity than they jumped the younger females.
I found her one day tipped on her back in a shallow hole,
unable to right herself, paddles waving.

Before going to work I stand outside the house
and watch through the dusty window
as she rises from her corner with swaying neck,
waddles to the pellet trough and fills her crop.

Eyesight failing, oil gland dry, feathers bedraggled,
she squats in her corner of the house most of the day
while the others attend to business. Every morning
we expect to find her still. This, we know,

will be her last summer. She's learning pain,
teaching herself death. She's dreaming of
bright places she's seen and of swimming in May
with brothers and sisters in the seasonal pond.

Control, power, secrecy

The day began with a boat trip before dawn.
I couldn't get warm. After the light increased
I saw doors on the houses along the shore.

I took the long walk home, a hot bath,
allowed myself a smile, and lay down;
she wiped the tears from my eyes,

scooped a desert under my ribs,
then left. In the evening I walked the dog
down along the raw outcropping, debris

of a mile-thick glacier, to the sea
where I remembered the fourth word:
possession.

I had supper with my father and mother and we
talked of where we would live next, each of us,
and what death would mean. Possession has in it

a vein of death. My father's last words,
as I left their house in pitch night: *Don't fall
into the ditch.*

The pain was enormous.
I limped home under clouds that hid
a nearly full moon, and slept well.

Fitful

When I wake it's three in the afternoon. She might
have come in and left again. Would I know?

I don't want to see my white feet, so sit a long time
on the edge of the bed, head down, eyes shut,

till I know what it is, the robin shape and blur
in the middle of the glass, and feel damaged. Smack.

No whisky in the kitchen, no courage, nothing to carry
me through one more day to the next. So. She finally knows me

well enough not to come home. I open the window but
grow tired of birds. Night enters the house as it always has.

The doors tell me nothing. Her T-shirts folded on the shelf,
sock and underwear drawers full. The house feels

as lonely as headlights breaking the sky.

General conditions

A storm woke me in the night
and I stood in the doorway facing
the mix of cold and warm air, wind
full of rain, trees full of wind, to see a
woman driving away. In the top part

of my body, the top part of my head,
I tried to find rain pants, yellow slicker,
gear for pursuit or survival. Normal
life, cupboards and shelves and dark corners of
the house briefly lit by the electric

muscle of memory, I tried to keep a
straight face, while thunder rumbled and trees
flung branches and the woman drove away,
rain so hard the dog whimpered loud
and louder.

Goodbye

The shut shut shutters told me when I got
home from school that Auntie Dora was dead after
two weeks stinking up our house and going to bed
forever in the spare room. Costs a lot to know
what's finished.

So we reach a resolution. My ex keeps the truck,
I keep the stereo and TV. We share the house where
our dog died and no children came
thank God. She wanted a new body
to hold, which wasn't what I had
in mind.

I've a blind spot to prevent me from knowing
the end. She wants to travel, loves sleep, loves
food. Fine. She wants the bed and table. Fine.
Once she loved food and bed and me,
no one else.

Guts. They stop the throat. Here's something
to remember: seven seconds to calm down, one
to draw the sword, sever the knot, step back
and mourn Auntie Dora. Won't rest till I'm in
love again.

Heart room

When does monogamy become celibacy? When
the skies have been grey for days and you stop

losing things. When the robin strikes the window
and stands panting on the ground
for longer than your anxiety to know

the outcome. As soon as it's clear. (To the bushes
to die. Into the air to test his wings.) As soon
as you forget. When does

celibacy become unfaithfulness? When
the child returns home to a gaunt house
in the shade of full-leafed trees. When

the wind sighs its way
along a city street and gives
you a sore throat.

When the smell of earth wakes sadness,
and your frantic self contracts with this dark cousin
to share the day if she will share the night.

As soon as it's clear. (To sit
on the house steps. To go in.) As soon
as you forget. There is mercy

in love but you are not patient. Pebbles
in the pocket. Count them. The iron bed. Tap.
Tap. Squeak of the wood stove door at dawn.

Hope Bay

1

Five freighters anchor off Hope Bay in the rain.
Five babies in my dream. I want something
interesting in the sky over America, currants and
nuts, coconut and rind, the tang of Christmas.
O list to port, face south. Hide out in the kitchen.

Five generators fill the night with humming.
The house is empty. Rusted barbed wire,
coiled, half-buried, has lost its purpose,
not its bite. A soft white zested orange
in one stung hand. Where does this come from?

A fence to keep the dog in, another to keep
the horses; this cake for a family feast.
What will we do for Christmas?
I'm afraid
of losing her, so many lost already.

Steve McQueen, for instance, on a motorbike,
breaking for freedom. I want–that field
unfenced! Love, I break for you.
She has to know she can be alone
so what she chooses will see her clearly.

2

Grandma showed me a robin's nest
in a dense green bush in her garden.
Inside the house lived her smell,
a hush, doors that clicked shut.
A bungalow haunted by what

I never saw. Tonight is calm.
I speak words. I sing,
listen for her voice, remember
the robin's nest. How can air stay
unjostled? I have not kept

ahead of loneliness. I kept
my wife. She gave me
the breast of all possibility. I lost
the breast and chance
got lost too.

3

The freighters turn. I
pick up baby after baby. Where is the
face I love? Grandma
Chadwick. A drop of rain on the head.
No one at the door. It may

snow tonight. All's new on this path.

In the living room in summer

She's pointing out a landmark
and I'm trying to close the window.

We're not talking. I'm praying and
she's biting back fresh words. Though

we seem to be talking together
my prayers are to a spirit that seems closer
since I shut the window and ended

the shrill crickets, and her words are so
hot she'd be shamed by them were they

ever spoken. Though we live together,
there is a fire near Paradise. She blames me
for nothing, that's all finished, and

I'm not blaming myself. The mark is nothing
to do with land, and with the window

shut we don't smell the smoke until
she is leaving and I'm no longer
bent on revenge.

New Year

If we do not sleep together by March then we will break apart.
Now is the first. Now the second. Now the third. Now the fourth.
If we do not lie down together, you wanting me, I you,

we will break apart. Now is the fifth. Now the sixth. Now
the seventh. Now the eighth. The sun shines and you're angry.
        I'm scared
to plan our lives, nothing left out. So we map our hunger

and walk to the nearest town. Now the ninth. Now
roses bloom in January:
and poppy, calendula, azalea.

Now that we are

Now that we are celibate a sickness is on the world.
Fish show up at board meetings, hackles raised,
demanding a return to the sea;
roofers sit on top of houses and spin creation
jokes; commuting is safe, dull

work accompanied by the scent of freesias. This
seems bad. Waiting for the car to warm up, I watch
crows swoop under the overpass till a homeless
Santa tosses a holly wreath from the railing, lights
a cigarette and vanishes. The wreath bounces on the hood,

my coffee spills. I sit still a long time, listening
to the traffic roar, a hand wet between my thighs.
One sunset by the sea, near the village where I grew up,
I cried my eyes out. I knew the sky by heart, the cliff
path, each villager, wanted them to see more clearly

their own lives. I stand with my mother father and sister,
sheltered from the wind by a remnant wall and
watch the waves rise broad and black; then
return to the dark green holly spines, the empty day,
let out the clutch, cross chaos into thin light.

Shortcut

I have found a path to stray from
and straying, feel the loss. These
crazy roots, wind-scattered twigs
and deadfall over moss are
the complications of life. Also
this money, that house, her lover,
my childhood, our sex, this fight.

It all tumbles in my eyes, dizzying. Sky's
evening matches morning's hue.
The leaves I thought were dead are
dying yet. Grey, I tell the forest, grey
marks the dead from the living. It will be
some time before a winter breeze kills
these last green beautiful days.

Songs the voice heard

Any moment it will stop
raining. My calves ache from
the crazy run from home and I

raise my head like any mammal
and my gut won't kiss me,
not even goodbye. O

the mud, the storm. I'm asleep
on my feet as never before.
There's a beckoning pattern in the distance

of clouds over the south field, rain
on this heavy heart. I don't want
remarkable pain,

though its twin is light. Listen.
Staple guns bang up coloured
bulbs all round the village.

Girls hang over the swollen river
to wash their festival dresses.
The valley trembles and

welcomes me back, though I
think I've not been here
before. What magic has tricked me

this time? I ran away and found
the doorstep of my first house
in a country I loved,

its people and animals
joined together in music
I can't hear unless I sing too.

This longing

I took care of sex during the day
and she took care of it at night.
At night I couldn't see.

Fuck off, I told her.
I have been paying attention.
I've been practicing.

She said I hurt her by my absence. Well
I spent a lot of money on therapy, but if that's
how she felt–

She gets that look and takes to
the middle of the room. There's shadows
near the walls. Even so

she can't even write her goodbye
and mine is so full of mistakes that I can't
read it when it's time.

Such a strong smell of sulphur, dirt devils
twisting and shade marrying brilliance.
Gotcha, says a voice.

I'm useless, she's stupid, then she's useless
and I'm stupid. We agree
we don't ever want to go back.

Twin beds in the Bath Y

1

Clematis and buddleia, one white pigeon
on the Pulteney Bridge.

I walk west out of town along the Avon
and meet a young woman "ohnen bustenhalten"
–to use Stegner's *Repose* expression, how coy–
pushing a baby in a pram, and she reminds me
of the first woman I slept with. My
fingers remember her skin, my eyes
the eyes of any beloved, always young.

Our faces now aren't so young:
mine in the mirror, yours turned
away. Accept it. It is what it is. "Try,"
is what the book on Zen said at Waterstone's last
night when I couldn't find a tissue and
my nose wouldn't stop dripping and you
wouldn't stop reading poems. It is what it is.
This before I took to the narrow bed at the Y,
with vitamin C and a book about Jesus.

And still we haven't had sex beyond
the shores of the New World.

You crossed the room
to your own bed
all night long.

2

I sit on the banks of the Avon and watch barges
till the black-haired girl in jeans and blue tank top
has passed in silence, all muscle and rounded limb
continuous with the day, warm, muggy
overcast. After the mother and child
a duck paddles by. Air's full of
distant traffic. The scent of buddleia and roses and
blackberries gone soft drifts through the willow's
trailing branches. Sun comes out and a fly lands
on my right shoulder. And by the barge *Electra*,

maroon! I'm in love, in Bath on Avon in September,
last year of this thousand, with the mother,
her nipples and skinny darkness,
tight-wrapped, fierce.

What is it that I haven't said to you whom I hold
dearest and longest? What have I not said to myself?

It has to happen somewhere, last love. So
(clematis and buddleia, one white pigeon)
we meet as arranged under the Pulteney Bridge,
eat quiche and stout, then back to the room.
I'm anxious to walk again, south along
the canal to the next village, but you
persuade me to stay with kisses, and all
afternoon we fuck on your bed and I come
once inside, once out. And it's good-
bye, farewell, though we don't know it yet.

When she told me

When she told me she'd slept with someone she
said it as though I already knew. I had to go
back to before gunpowder. Had to learn to use
my hands. The airport was an open field farmers
had abandoned, a few trees in full leaf, cow pies,
birds I'd never heard. After a long anxiety,

sun rose above the east ridge snagged by high
branches and ground mist melted. When she told
me I saw my first enemy and had time to turn
the sword's thrust and was cut only. When
she spoke again I had no time to fend, no chance
to dodge and the blade went deep. The blade

goes deep and all time is pain. And the miracle
of loss. The blade withdraws. Because I'm alive
the sword is mine. The flesh is mine. The blade,
the valley, the airport, the pain, the light, her life,
all belong to me and I'm silent. Fallen with the freshly
fallen.

Love has eaten us

Beloved, you are there at my death.
The wind blows through it, mist rising
as the day brightens. In this clearing

I'm seeing the beautiful parts of the world
collide and I'm dying, every moment
a greater sadness and clarity.

That day we drank wine and ate bread
at Pagliacci's, the children lit candles. At our
table a girl burnt her fingers. Your face

bent over mine, happy to see me. Never
seen one so lovely. The children around us now
were with us then. All is as it was as

we pass through again. We are this, and
on the other side of night waits the sleeping
lion no longer hungry. We are this, and

what I'm leaving is you, and what you're
grieving is me, and what we're giving up
is nothing.

Ferry

I can't wade ashore now, in the dusk of a winter day. Waves lap
yellow logs at the water's edge, dark trunks. I'd love a night beyond
that tree line, half wanting company, half a cage to keep me tame

hunkered among roots the water sips, sips. The self I'm falling for
and the self I'm leaving: mainland, island. Two fires. Home and away.
The north, yes, intellect. But the south pole, there's a licorice stick,

there's a lollipop. A black horse rides from the mountains, big and full
of wind, winter fur a halo of spines. He's the side of the world
that covers the sun, the one on the path when I went fishing with

my dad. The horse nods his head and mist gathers on the stubble of
his nose. His knees buckle. He lowers his body, crouches. I'm not
surprised when the whale breaches; the whale breaches; call it

fish, horse, we never caught it. No. I want to bear myself with grace
where a voyage meets disturbance and something rises, slippery
or seeming so.

After the ice age

1

On Garry Oak Meadow we
rose in summer dark
and walked to the donut shop

with Spirit, our setter cross.
At dawn the tracks of
animals were too many

to count, T-shirts and jeans were
enough to keep us
warm, the graving-dock cranes lit

salt mist on the harbour, and
we were happy. The
tenth year we sailed to the island

of snakes in hot July, fenced
a garden against deer,
chose weapons, took positions:

she claimed the garden and all
it produced, I claimed
the wood stove and all the trees.

In our house on the hill, in
front of the fire,
as the valley filled with snow,

we made war. As the valley
filled with ice our fingers
wove, long nights, body against

body, a myth. When Spirit
died I carried him
to shore, put him on a boat.

2

So we've come out of the cold,
we've left the valley.
Where can I go, my old dog?

3

Ah. Blue life. Half a muffin.
April sun. Rain between
clouds and wet trees. I walk the

street, my heart in sync with some
old traveller heart,
but at home the blizzard still

rages. Afternoon's like night,
the sky very black.
Two letters arrive, one is

a wedding invitation.
How has this happened?
How on earth has this happened?

4

Also the divorce papers.
It's too dark right now.
I pack my things and go back

to England, my cousin's vows.
His ten-year-old step-
daughter draws me. I look like

a convict. She sits easy
on my lap under
canvas after the guests leave

and we listen to rain on
cloth and geese honking
low over the blue slate roofs.

5

I love that dark green garden,
smell of summer rain,
holding a child, white and cold,

my heart broken, the worse part
thrown away. I love
too this blue life, the best half,

a brand new boat with wings. True,
next day at breakfast
we drink another bottle

of champagne, why not? Marriage
is a gift, their love
will go far, far as it can.

I think maybe I'm human,
I tell my cousin,
the world's newest animal.

In morning light a hawk drifts
high above our heads
amid white clouds and blue sky.

Battlefield

Death of a samurai

Agony

It is to death I turn, the ways
it can happen and what it's like
in battle, on an epic scale:
choreography that–flame
thrower, machine gun, missile–gentles
each soldier's muddle
with each enemy soldier.
Buddies dying, remote
beloved borne like a charm
into each advance. Loss
of life: loss of the image of home.

❧

Mifune I loved as a boy. His sword
will reverse chaos. O broken life.

❧

His legs, folded under him, are still,
skin already grey, blood hard and black.
His eyes open and his chest fills,
empties, his fingers swipe at
sticky threads. A terrible clatter: heart
wants out. Am I ready for the slack
sides of his neck to flutter like dark
pennants of men hungry for that?

Samurai

When Mifune Toshiro fell it was not to his knees but
grace took him down, staccato sorrow, the body toppling
in a medieval garden amid the noise of the last battle,
the swift sad motor abbreviating his life insisting: he
will not die, will never die. Ferocity and surprise confuse
his young face. There will be no resolution but death. Rain

is an idea at the bottom of my heart. Undisturbed,
floating, November remembers itself missing
from the light. I can't get away. I can't get to it,
though I'm here, nearly drowned. It's awful when pain is
what you want to hang on to. When Mifune falls he believes
in body inventing for itself the future. There's another

body waiting, say in the shadows of the stark gleaming
plum, that has nothing to do with past or future, that
is outside the war. Between her and Mifune (still falling)
dwells one moment. The sword has severed image from
beauty in one clean cut. Alongside Mifune's anxiety–image
chafing body–lies his heart, a jewel, anxiety's lesson.

Vancouver from England

I love Mifune, the roll of his shoulders, the way
his eyebrows arch. A new boy from England,
I watch samurai movies, learn a wave man is
a masterless warrior: an exile, no one
to tell him what to do, no one. In 1969, January,
a dark month, I lose my accent, practice leaping
shadow to shadow to peer into windows,
a spy not yet sure what the mission is.
The rest of the year necessary to unfold
Mifune Toshiro's walk, never quite seeing
what's there or knowing how to do what he does.

I see him go down, simple as that, in one motion,
from standing to sitting, from engagement to
stasis, as if he's stepped from outside to inside,
from the cold night of thieves and brigands to
a warm fire and soup and a fresh straw bed.
His whole body alert, then in a kind of dream.
A collapse brought on by war, wounds from
previous campaigns, agony, surrender. So fast.

He invites me to climb a tree to gather plums.
We sleep together under a black sky with
a scattering of stars, the Milky Way, precarious
in the branches. Mist shrouds the dawn.
One day, he says, I'll die. By noon
his pain has to hold stillness. Already
rain has begun to fall. My muscles ache
from clinging to slippery wood as I wait
for *him* to fall.

I love Mifune

He has killed this man. Already among the possible
future women a river of light meanders, and he sees
he will not die, will never die until he's found her.
There will be no more rain. No more clouds. No more
winter. His heart is nearly drowned, hanging onto pain,
unable to rise to take a look. What's in the river?
A betrayal of the present. Who waits in the shadow
of the temple wall? Vague figures like trees.

It was in the autumn, it must
have been, as little as he remembers,
perhaps he remembers that. And what the fight
was about and which war and whether
the men were samurai or monks.

Anxiety has nothing to do with the past or the war
or what will happen soon. He asks for more life.
A day or two, just a week of no pain, time to say
goodbye. He asks for life. No consent. The moment
of taking someone's future dissolves the image of
taking. No permission. Follow the last breath. Next
to trapped recklessness beauty lies. Follow beauty.

Apprentice

If you head down a steep grade
and dislodge a stone–stop and wait
till the stone stops rolling. Mark its
resting place before you continue;

avoid that place, it's already used up.
A stern yet playful man, famously
accurate, a glint in his eye, he said:
I'm not so interested in fighting, but in

doing it without holding tight to loss.
He said, The way through each battle is
to remain perfectly still. He said,
Watch your step *there's blood everywhere,*

then used his blade to cut the warrior
from the beautiful being–and in one
quick lesson this apprentice was severed
from his beloved. Geese cross overhead,

horizons wobble. A woman, patient with age,
collects windfall apples and pears past ripe.
I remember a road, the hills and turns,
England, a fool and his knight.

Last battle

All night prayers at the temple. No lamp oil lit.
The lieutenant of the outer palace guard, left
division, is a brave warrior, Mifune says. Since
he intervened in the matter of my prosecution
for treason, I owe him my life. He sent priests
to row me from the island. Mist on still water.
Shrouded rock. At the beach a boy to hand
me straw sandals. My wife at the shrine.

In the dark we wait for the council to arrive.
I want Mifune Toshiro to talk about the fight
because I'm afraid and cold, but he will
not speak of this war except to say,
Solitude is a distillation of wildness.

Our forces are great! cries a voice. Our
Lord is great! Our men are hungry for battle!

Count my arrows, says Mifune, and when you've counted,
count again. Murderous events are foretold for tonight,
the sixth of the ninth month.
And while I smooth each shaft,
the warriors exchange poems, as always.

Tired from yesterday's march and victory our
vast enemy's unprepared for a dawn attack.
In great surprise they whirl in the temple garden
like leaves in accidental formation, fight
like men with nothing to lose.

Once, he says, when I was a child
and gravely ill, I knelt at a window
and watched other children play
in the snow. Now I sit with my blood
falling out, my son and wife dead, my men
giving chase to the last enemy soldiers.
Hoarfrost still beards every branch and
berry, and I still can't bear to withdraw.

Last words

Deer came in the night, he says, soon
there'll be wasps and crows.
West of Japan is China.
You should take Buddhist vows.
My heart's exhausted.

Birds unwind and lift
into the sky. Outside
the temple it's nearly morning,
the ninth month, the air
gold, the music made

by monks at prayer.
West is metal. You will want
my sword, he says.
Five positions only. Remember.
Center, right, left, up, down.

Damage the enemy. Take
the wound with honour.
Don't hide in doorways,
keep the light behind you.
Know a song or two.

When a samurai breaks
his sword he crosses the sea
to China to die. But first
thing every morning
he cuts a paper rose.

The noise of their industry

He falls down in a garden. It seems like a garden.
Yes, it's a garden. So used to stepping over deadfall, he listens
for wild life, gauges the position of sunrise beyond
the forest, but is confused by careful hedges, the subtle

paths that when followed allow, vista by vista,
a cumulative experience of nature bound. Always
disturbing, his experience of gardens:
the plum tree under which his first lover waits; paths

mown between graves; the royal hedge maze he can't
find his way through. Garden or not, he's cross-legged
on wet ground. Cold soaks into his clothes. Chill blood
on his skin. He's wounded. He is hit. I'm struck

by the way he has fallen–not flat on his face, neither
back nor forward, to one side or the other, but vertically,
spine straight, face tilted up. What concerns the tall trees
around him, crucial to him, is his way of dying.

Their branches will outleaf him now, native or
planted won't matter. He is what? Feeling
sick? Glad to be outside and alone? This home's
not the one he left his mother. As for the trees, they

don't trouble him, whoever they are. They gently
monitor, intent on their work, never glance at him
cross-legged on the ground. A humming sways in and
on the air. He listens and follows the girl in white

as she backs into the green dark. She must lean forward
to smudge his forehead. *This one.* It's raining. *This one.*
Wilderness is not his ordinary experience of gardens.
He didn't hear the bell struck. Nor the note's end.

Grace

When I try to find Mifune
falling, in films already seen,
some moments come close, some fights
look like that fight, some sets look right,
the way the trees hang their leaves as if
under a sudden downpour,
a building in the background that might
be a temple. But the image in my head
has played so often that it's antique,
and what I want to extract from
Mifune, the fallen warrior,
must be somewhere else. Outside
a different temple, in other woods,
in the sound of any large gong.

Say this house, a plain farm neglected
because it's of stone and difficult
to burn and will afford shelter should retreat
prove necessary. This house reminds us of home,
its survival an omen already. Stark
against the sky it has something to say
about the dwellers of this land, ghosts all,
who, like us, require a symbol
to gain their way to heaven.

And we know this by heart: the home
we've made of earth, the contract
between us and heaven that we'll seal,
once we're settled, with beeswax and gold,
has its blue counterpart in the afterworld.
We'll rest here on our last journey. Outside's
windy, bright, too empty. To die in the open
hurts the soul. We dead want nothing
but the ordinary furniture of a room:
fireplace, chair, door, table, window, bed.

Lesson

Two workmen argue beside a half-built stone wall.
The samurai steps forward to give me the carving–
a beautiful woman with smooth golden arms–
the best he's ever done. Night enters the long valley

in the shape of purple clouds. A shadow by my foot.
Before I react, his sword flashes and cuts the snake
in two and the tail vanishes into a hole. He picks up
the head and smiles. I can't believe my eyes.

We are saying goodbye. A man, fierce and lonely,
one of the workers, wants to fight me. We stand
face to face. I tell him how much I love and will
miss Mifune Toshiro, my teacher, and he starts to cry.

Mifune sits quietly against the wall looking at us.
The wounded snake coils at his collar bone, about to strike.
The fierce man squats before me to ask something.
This is really goodbye because the chorus begins.

Well/Spring

When Mifune Toshiro falls it is not to his knees, no.
In the silence between attacks he falls into a lotus–his
torso erect, gaze taking in the plum trees–and
a revelation: The last battle outside the temple will be
announced by five notes of the village gong.

Last night we took a long walk, stopped at the well
for a drink of water, in the courtyard for the blessing
of a priest. Rain, the monk says, is too swift and sad
to fully comprehend. The samurai says, I will not
die, will sacrifice everything. He smiles.

A terrible thirst remembers itself as he falls
through dark trees, in the stillness between attacks.
Pain is all you have to hold. When Mifune falls
he knows that victory does not concern him, that

there's another drama, a woman waiting in
the shadows, a woman in white, her face
clear, unwritten, beautiful. He has mistaken
others for her often. Between her waiting

and Mifune falling, is one still moment.
Between what's outside him and inside
her, between his violent descent and her
will, is a mechanism that will solve time.

Already among the fighters sleeping and
the already lost a river of light meanders, and
though neither he nor she sees it, one thinks: water
and the other: joy; and thirst begins to trouble both.

The Sutler

sutler, n. Camp-follower selling provisions etc. to soldiers.
[f. obs. Du. *soeteler* f. *soetelen* befoul, perform mean duties]
Concise Oxford Dictionary. Fifth Edition

The Sutler

There's a pause in the battle to clear the bodies
and I'm amazed to hear the pips and trills
of chickadees. What am I
to make of this, on the run
between corpses? I'm not ready
for the cow in my path, flanks steaming, still
alive, breath large. On either side, slain men give birth
to entrails. With sun through smoke the land's
in profoundest glory with everything
too late to speak and no one to listen.
Stories can't touch this. Hark–
a bass note from the core of the world. I am alive!

"All aglow in the rue the rue the rue of rats," says Stephen
when we're back in the trench. Joe the drunk calls me ticklecuff;
he'd make a pickpocket too, except he's thick as pitch. "Oy! You sir!"
says Lol. "There's blood in this ditch and a worm up your arse."
"Nick us some stuff from the stiffs," says Simon, "there's a love."
"Magnificent killin, spillin, a cup of grace, that last charge," says
        Stephen.
"Watch it, Stevie-boy," says Brinley, "night's closing in."
"But don't worry lads," says Stephen, "thy foe is half mist and
half smoke, thy enemy's the bottle and thy new wife's bloke."
"Aye," I say. And all you must do is think
what I'll take when you're dead
on the field and pray it doesn't happen.

In the pockets are rabbit's feet and stones and
locks of hair, apple seeds, rooster feathers,
St Christopher, a pouch of dirt, a broken
silver chain, coins, a nest of ribbons, a piece of
green silk, china shards, and sometimes nothing.
I'm used to the work. The blunted weapons, the armour,
the trinkets, the keepsakes. Their bodies still dressed
in soft brown clothes seem part of the earth; it's easy
to see they'd vanish in time. I take the boots,
leaving a pasture of feet no longer sore, glad
for the warm coat I found, glad they're not alone, not
in pain. How much blood the soil must swallow!

That donkey trotted out of the trees, a great event
because we thought he'd been killed. The donkey
came from nowhere weeks ago and we put him
to work pulling timber and carts of guns and
shells and it became a habit to stroke his
nose at night and find him grain and straw
and it was a famous day when he appeared across
the field because although I'd not seen him
killed or found his body I thought him dead,
and we gathered round to welcome him home and
took turns brushing his coat and slapping his neck
and exclaiming how thin he was and lucky.

I was only in the countryside once before I came
to try my luck at war and was as frightened then by ducks
as I am now by noise of battle. I had in those days
never seen a man opened up and one morning
I shot a stag with a borrowed rifle. The sky
so blue afterwards, the trees of the little wood leaning
close, the smell of grass and taste of iron. Wounds are
like flowers or suns or black twig nests. In the torsos of men
I see the blossom or eclipse or egg, as if the body
is only a place to find such things. My skill
at lifting jewels and watches and rings without
grazing the skin has come in handy.

At mealtimes there's a sense of order amid chaos,
never enough time to finish. One sweet and grainy dish
I push behind the rag curtain where I keep
my treasures so the others won't see. We stop and
listen to the creak of a machine being hauled, a
sapper stretching wires over the earth. It's nearly
dark. I know every rut and root of this hole
blindfold. And what of that time in the country,
the stream I used to wash in and the little waterfall?
A whole unwritten part for me to play that had
all the shine of a healthy life and died on the lips
of the lad I was, who I cry for now. All

was corrupted before my coming here,
then all was corrupted further by the war.
Look at Lol shivering against his cigarette,
not trying to eat, too jumpy to sleep, ready
to take a wound if not lose a limb. And
Wilf and Simon will meet at midnight for
the spice and home of each other. We're haunted
by the ones we fear to lose, though it's ourselves
who will be lost. Death has hemmed us in yet
night still fills with stars while in the soil
a forest grows and from the highest branches birds
sing up blue sky and a stiff breeze. Many tales

I hear from men who can't sleep and
need others to know what fine lives they've had.
Tonight's Brinley's turn: *After church we used
to slide down yellow dunes between the gorse and the
sea on sand so hot we'd be up yelling murder*. His voice
sings. I close my eyes. This land too was beautiful
when we came, pasture against the grain, grain to the forest,
now it's all stubble and shattered branches. I'm not
ready to die. Most men think that. Most will be
dead before long. I wish each of them a long life and
years of hard work on his own land. They frown.
What I do terrifies them worse than the next battle.

Such pretty faces some have, unmarked
by age or sun, unharmed by what killed them:
metal going in, blood slipping out. They died
fast. Those who live longer wear masks of
awe. And even when the head is destroyed,
the body is worth a glance: the hand
that was a baby's once still
soft and clean against the mud, blue
veins under the skin of a thigh, pale
belly fringed by coils of hair. O my lovely
breath and the new wind, and the laughter
from both sides of the field as the sun comes out.

My task is not to carry the dead or finish off
the dying, stanch the flow of blood, find
the missing limb, close the eyes or say a prayer, heed
a final word or lay my hand upon a brow. I know
when men are dead and won't touch the wounded.
I won't fight or run away or keep the fire lit or
dig the pit or fill it in again. I press the evidence of
one life against my palm, save
the good luck others leave behind–
a mother's face, sweetheart's kiss, a tarnished ring
and sundry bits of home. I'm cosy with the remnants
of those who cursed me yesterday. This morning

I crawled through earthworks,
in and out of foxholes across the field, till I forgot
it was day or night, and when the peace exploded–
chickens scrabbling at broken sod–I laughed so hard
I fell on my back. Along came thrushes with little listening faces
to pull at worms. I'm followed
by my father, I think, who can no longer speak,
while Mum sings songs she made up herself, how
they had me as a last resort, away was where
they wanted to be and will be now I'm good
as dead. No, that's wrong. I've got it wrong.
I'm the one lost. Dad died

one autumn afternoon between the five o'clock
whistle and the sooty night, a time when families
breathed a bit before tea, and Mother joined him
the next year as quiet as a mouse after cooking potatoes
and setting the curtains on fire. I hope
the chickens and wild birds find safe trees
away from the war. I look back on the girl I loved
as if losing someone couldn't happen
in a country with a name. I look ahead into
no man's land where men meet
for the last time. This is what is meant,
I suppose, by sadness and what is meant by

glory. It's better that no one confides in me, it eases
my job, frees me to see the pattern the boys make
together as they go and later as they lie
where they've fallen. By not caring for one
I care for them all and keep an eye on the weather,
the geese and crows, the ancestors who roam
the field with me at dusk and dawn, and feel
how quiet it was here once, how the wind blew,
how seas came and went and a thousand thousand
creatures died and a thousand thousand
came to life and how all of it will happen
again. Joe leans against a stanchion, not drunk,

pulling at his cigarette. He fancies he's an arcade
hero welcomed home, a game one. "Ticklecuff,"
he murmurs when I catch his eye. Look at him
dance from foot to foot on the frozen ground to calm
his mind. Death is close. The happiness
they think they want, these lads, out of reach, over
the next hill, they discover last thing before sleep.
It is close. The ember at his pursed lips. One more
puff, my son, then turn out the light, don't
forget your God bless, and God bless yourself
for standing there and me for seeing you, and
all the stars like a blanket spread over us.

The donkey went out with a night patrol and
the boys returned without him. He's nothing
this morning, a big lump on the field
in only his brown fur and big ears and
a hole in one side, his nose cold and hard,
the velvet gone, an old donkey covered
by frost, each rib on his barrel chest
a little white frozen wave. It's a long time
since he was a colt in a paddock with his first
taste of grass–before I was born.
When animals die in our service
a wildness in us is lost. The first

snow fell last night and our trench looks brand new and
there's a house. Snow on the roof, smoke from the chimney.
Not far away but a killing distance. We've been dug in
since high summer and never seen the house before.
Who lives there still? How has a house survived our
onslaught? Cinder path to the front door. Holly bush full
of berries beside the path. In the window a child's face
stares out over the broken ground as a bell chimes the
hour. A fox approaches the garden gate, his tracks dainty
in the snow; as if we are the passing dream and he is real;
after he stops to sniff the air he looks back
at me and a bugle sounds the next attack.

All day the snow fell and melted on my skin. Brinley
Morris had a poem folded in his pocket, ideas
of what we were doing and what might happen
to him–pretty true in hindsight. How well
his limbs fit together. Men are built much the same,
splayed fingers, gentle toes, guts and bones between.
The writing was a child's. *Lots of times I come
back to the trench and feel I belong here. This is
home, this patch, these are my brothers. We
return and the corner of dirt welcomes us.*
And what do I feel? I am a thin thief in a great-
coat, more curious every day about the changes

in men on the battlefield. A bleeding rabbit drags
its grey body over the snow. The boys rise up
out of the trench bristling with the promise of something
they can't speak. Exhausted, they shovel a new tunnel
in the ground, using picks to break the frozen sod,
their lantern hearts choked with light our enemies can't
see and should they see would serve to unveil their own.
For what I find in enemy uniforms is the same.
The difference between our men and theirs can't
be measured: how can you tell where a word
comes from? At the centre of stone is darkness. I love
to watch a man's body come home from fighting.

Tomorrow arrives on the shoulders of contraptions
that do not depend on horses and haven't the beauty
of living things. An explosion throws us back before
bidding us closer. Flares light each snowflake
and make an echo of shadows on the already fallen.
Nothing looks meek. Any trail is the child of
tricky parents who make all the sense
in the world then rest, having already fallen
in love and battle. I'm flabbergasted by the trembling
valley. How can we cause this? False thing. Lightning.
River. A bell chimed from a church on the far hillside
every night last week.

I'm only half killed when all the rest are dead,
not curious any more about wounds and
pockets or whether I'll die or live, till
one lad waves his arm and I lift him
onto my back. The waterfall. The stag. The pool
of blood. I have fallen into a new country.
That goodbye day the harbour water was dark,
my sweetheart's coat spotted with rain.
Her shoulders shook as she crossed the street
and later it snowed. We trudge all night from
field to field, over each stone wall, the sky above us
full of crows and nothing on the horizon to spoil

the calm of his pale face. I empty our pockets,
leave everything behind, even night and
the stars that make a final map. I've seen
the likes of this before. This path. This tree.
I've always wanted to carry someone.
To do it right takes a long time.
There's no neat and tidy way. Maybe
all of us have the guts in the end.
There's no trouble. Just a bit of a breeze
off the smoking plain, dawn air with a tremor,
the smell of grass–a kind
of falling through milky sky.

When the sun comes up I stop beside a narrow track
and put the boy on the grass. Ravens click and caw
in an oak tree above. The moss under his head gleams;
little cups on the ends of thin stems hold water drops.
I'm scared to move and lose this place. My face warms
with the day and the chest pain dulls. I can't be lost.
When the girl and I met long ago. When we met. When
we met I felt an ache big enough to hold the sea.
What a sunny day now. What a sunny day. I left her
in winter. Just a roar of traffic and the kick
of a massive gun. The boy's eyes so big, planted
in breath as long as it lasts. Now the birds start to sing.

The rising body

The rising body

The birds in August sing in
a fog of trees and
I stand in the porch
and think: God: Job: skirt, rain:
the smoothness is mine. Then:

spy: dream: the roughness
uncut, the splendour
of God waiting in the dark for
Job's rant. I get breathless
at the thought of what's beneath

(I spoke to you by phone,
you were in a hotel room
the heat turned high)
and what's above
all these facets, all this pulse.

Tell me true,
tell me love,
if I for answers came to you
you'd smile, but will
you show me how to leave?

I'm crazy tonight from chocolate
and green tea, trying to incubate
a dream I barely recall about you:
we were in love, I held back. Now
rain on leaves lets me go.

After the divorce

It's quiet now, June.
Looking both ways I cross

the valley floor, cross
my heart hope to die, and

hear only the slosh of bourbon
in the flask. Not a bird,

only the click of tin rusting
underfoot. Beside the path each tree

hunts the same light. I follow
the small river

at the end of the green trail
on whose far bank

the year's milky foxgloves
tilt sinister; the path curves right.

I stagger, ankle deep, into
the water. In strong sudden day

I don't know which side
of the world will fall.

Flash in the pan

A girl fell in love with me, then a woman, then a man.
A junky gave me a fish. My own love was a winged
termite, dumb and happy in blazing air after months
of darkness. Then I was in love with a woman who

loved me in a cottage near the sea. We talked nonstop,
heard freight trains blow, smelled brine when the fog
rolled in. Because I was afraid to say what I wanted–
for her to turn over, wear chains, tell me what she wanted–

she slept with others. "If I lose you," I said,
"I lose everything. Again." I fell in love with a girl,
then another. A woman fell for me. I fell for a different
woman, then I fell for a friend, then his wife. His wife

fell for me. Then it all ended. Everything. O,
one more thing. I had a perfect green sweater and
a perfect pair of black shoes; I had brown cords;
I had them once, but then I set them on fire.

Before night

Children swing from monkey
bars, monks stitch prayer flags
and the wind blows in late afternoon,
as if the world could be
like that.

A fox dies in a girl's arms,
the click of its wings sharp
above the rustle of leaves.
It happened exactly, even
the wings, though long before

I knew it was strange. What
to make of death and longing
and the end of summer?
Away with this. I'll build
a baby out of snow.

Balloonists

Balloonists circle the earth, measure progress
in land kilometers, 44000, while bombs fall;
they say that hardly a night goes by
ungorgeoused by flame from some conflict.

I'm falling in love, sitting in the cab watching
sunset on Fort Street and listening to Bobby
Vinton sing *Blue Velvet*, "precious and warm
the memory through the years," and I catch myself,

catch myself, a glimpse of something brilliant,
extraordinary, that hated
being born, that screamed and pushed, yet loved
the gentle milk and long floating days of

being seen.

Prison life

I've been shot, thrown
off a plane, I've jumped
out a building, I had nothing
to lose. I liked the basement suite
because it was cool
in summer and the girl in the next

building never drew her blinds.
I wasn't looking, but she was
spackle and I was hot as hell. She
was a heartbeat away, across
the narrow path. I couldn't leave
myself alone in the dark. I forgot
the stove's spiral elements burning

red. She liked the single candle.
Outside, jaws waited for the moon,
and when it rose full I crept
out my window, through hers.

Months later, in the courtroom,
after she said what she said
had really happened, I realized
the itch had been mine alone.

Two years. I am not frantic
for escape or belonging. We
made contact; we transformed. People turn
into teachers. Do this, they say, pick a job,
wake up, go to sleep. Fear's amazing,
life's amazing, two years is nothing.

These seeds, a full jar

Every winter night she read catalogues in bed,
ordered the seeds next morning, celebrated their
arrival in spring. I grow sick at heart,

so many left, and my dream to scatter them, in hope
that one or two will germinate, no longer viable.
Their names stop me, the labels dated years ago

in her hand send me running for a cigarette.
I empty the packages one by one into a jar
and think it's done, isn't it, our dream? My fences,

her painted ceilings. The house felt lived in.
Reasons for organizing cupboards unfurled
in the middle of the night when one of us

reached for the other. Now the whole place
needs painting again. Let me tell you
how I failed her, how numb I feel. Tomorrow

I'll continue with the seeds, but today I need
to unpack the heavy blood that longs and longs and longs.
Our goodbye was too soon, not done, not whole.

(How could I know?
At the thought of us
I shy and hurt.)

At the rubbish heap

No flower here, not the season. But oak trees
from a remembrance of oak trees, a wedding party
of squirrels armed with acorns, snowberries,
and above all children in the sky.

And I have found a plank to sit on,
and sit on into evening,
head fuzzy with debt. *How long
will I love thee*? Till the sun warms my side
and choruses revolve
and I'm breathing
ginger fire.

When the sun has left the earth,
these kids (call them crows)
circle and circle, clever with the air,
and sing of home and sleep. They call
me to myself, these marrying crows,
to name what I've lost.

Midnight is the appointed hour.
It grows still. The plank is cold.
Invisible now, except when they cover stars,
the lovers wheel and murmur. None of us
know enough. There's nothing to know.

Behind the community centre

Children hang from monkey bars. The wind
rustles branches that fell in the night. As if

this could be lungs again. Blood. Native wit. All
together. Part of the fence is down and the wading

pool's full of leaves. A boy sits on a blue island
looking intently at his cut finger. Newsprint

blows across the basketball court. *Schools and*
prisons full. Latest advance in the treatment

of cancer. My dear cells, I am not old.
A thin man with blue eyes, I have held

doves, a woman, a dog, alive and dead,
now I tremble and wait below.

Last week my knees unlocked and I fell
open-mouthed in the dirt. Can you miss

what you've never had? O I miss
my kids!

I believed in things

Ah I loved her when she gave me the back street and I
 could whisk up a storm.
All gone.
The memory blocked the way the needle is by bone.
I don't want it.
The little child in the picture is me I guess, sweet kid,
kept me warm for years.
The hole left when I'm quiet at last
is room, and I'm waiting every night
for someone to register. Imagination I used to
imagine, holding my breath and counting till
light faded and colours quit, till air began to eat its tail,
was all it took. Think of a belly, think of a ball.
Now I'm afraid to want what I say.

Cousin

To get death out of the way say it first, then fall
from the highest branch of a tree
in England so hard breath's gone

and all that remains is a bud in the heart.
Two boys and my uncle's Alsatian
in the woods of Cheshire.

I remember agony, a stream hooked
round vivid grass, the shock of no breath.
This was the year before Crusader Camp

in Wales with double-oh-seven Bond James
Bond and O! the Crusades: *The Horror
Omnibus*, dozing on Sundays in a tent in Nefyn.

Clammy Norman churches where girls
in skirts decent by half an inch tripped over
cold flagstones that kept the buried from the living,

our cocks crying and crying after it was all
over. I remember grasping his while he grasped mine
and singing hymns after dinner then praying in silence.

Crescent Beach

Back to a time when the deepest jewels of the psyche were easily
woken.
What was that like?

Can't breathe; I lie in my bunk and listen
to the crew moaning as a summer
voyage ripens into nightmare and
the ocean turns to clay. I climb on deck

to a world shot with visions, wind
in the rigging a choir's broken
harmony and the captain a father who
won't admit to his children that

something terrible has taken place–
a drunk in church or a sane man
in bedlam. There's strange light in the sky
when the crew draw their swords.

All this happened long ago,
in the aftermath of a great war.
That last and bloody voyage I was
cast overboard with the officers

into the loamy flood. Just keeping our
heads was an ordeal of centuries. I recall
there was a trick to it: if you went back
to just before the war began and began again

you might catch a liquid current and float above
the worst battles, and have some control in your going.

Dry August

It's gritty these nights sleeping alone. The bed
you understand is clean: blue cotton sheets, high
thread-count. I dream Sahara women troubled
by the death of a chicken, digging up bones
in the garden, and I struggle briefly awake to
the cooler side, throw off the bolster, straddle
a fresh horse just out of colthood, sweep
ahead the sand till the horse
falls over the cliff to the beach
where armies await orders. Am I

to anticipate a marine invasion from the east or
a land-force from the south? What
is the meaning of the bones and dead bird?
My queen has left the counting house
barren as a winter nest, and the prime minister
says I must improve my public address.

All I have is what comes at night, and
the dust I wake to tells me
only that the well is dry.

Friday before work

I go out for a smoke.
It's evening all day this time of year
and I expect night

any moment. Other than that
there's nothing on my mind. I watch
a cricket climb through wet grass–never
to get dry, let alone survive till dawn–

who carries forward a dream
for the ones who sang all summer. Then
I go down to feed the chickens who roost
all day this time of year, and tell them

about the cricket. The colour of their feathers
opens an ache in my chest, dark rain
drums the roof of the coop, and when
the sun shines at the last moment

I turn and fix my gaze between
bristling hills and cashbox clouds.
I count the birds that have died.

Living alone

1

Out in the December crowds
this ache turns

into proof
that I miss someone.

They've finished
the overpass and fenced the window

with six round cement pillars.
The day ends laughing.

2

A year ago I bought her a ribbed shirt
that clung to her breasts and I leaned close

and shut one eye and ran a thumbnail over
the hills and down the valleys, took a breath

and changed sides. I told her to put nothing
in her pockets, wear no underpants, not

ruin the edge of her body like that.
The shirt lifted when she reached

a filter from the top shelf,
her belly button winked.

3

We arranged to meet at my favourite
boutique and I waited and waited

then came home and took the whisky
upstairs.

Everything always fit,
though she claimed it didn't.

4

She pulled on spandex and wool and
ran with her women friends while

men prowled the sidewalks, stood
behind every curtain of every house and

watched from cars as I jogged behind,
kept my distance, combed my hair,

and still in bloom on pale stems
were marigolds.

5

To the season's first cocktail parties she wore
the red silk gown. In church she wore

the shortest skirt. She hated skirts and gowns,
though I bought her many: they still hang

on my side of the closet, among the leather jackets,
those skins of scheming bats.

6

Ah, where to end. I gave her
a costume for solstice

to wear when the lights went out
and she flinched. All-night

crews were pouring cement.
After dinner we drank together,

listened to the clank
and roar of enterprise,

unable to leave,
unable to stay.

She put on coveralls and danced. A man
on a high crane saw her and danced back.

7

All this happened at the start
of winter, the quick darkest day,

as if possession led to bankruptcy,
as if everything I finished finished me.

Talisman

The bus so beautiful at
the highway crossroad swims
with October sun

and the people on board
gape. I know each one
will breathe a final breath,
their fingers touch a last roughness;
let it be bark.

Later, amazed again, I come
across a plastic parcel of guts
glistening pink on the side of the road,
innards from some truck spill, and
I'm a big animal on a hill in spring

moaning to hear myself moan
after a cold night before
the shelter-belt is mature.

After Seattle

The American woman rages
against what is done in her country's name.
She cries too easily against

what's done. Too easily, I think, she
condemns in herself what is strong.
I would like to say something

about the heart
of the bombed child. I would like to ask
Who has drunk blood?

Who has raped women?
Who has killed friends?
Who has burned villages?

I would like to say something.
Who will survive this?
I would like to say:

The imperial dream bombs itself.
Let the children go. Let the bombs
go. Ride them like Strangelove.

Too easily, I think, the American
woman condemns herself. And between
the blamer and the blamed

some small innocence is lost.

The sisters and the goat

Once upon a time two sisters waited
in an ice cave for day to empty around them.

While Blue Eyes stood still as a statue,
Green Eyes undressed her, touched each nipple,

kneecap and hip. Then Blue Eyes pretended
to faint and from the back of the cave,

out of the last darkness, trotted a goat,
a bone clenched between its teeth.

Green eyes looked into blue. The agreement
was no talking. What happened next

furnished the sisters with a secret they'd
share with no one, then blue eyes closed,

green eyes widened, the goat ran from the cave,
and all–bone of a child, child of a mother,

mother of a child, sister of a sister–lived
happily ever after, happily ever after.

Undersea Gardens

That winter I wore a wetsuit six hours a day and
swam with the seals. Once an hour I plugged
the shower nozzle to each wrist and filled my skin
with hot water. I swam with ratfish and sharks.

A girl's voice narrated from the submarine speaker
as I tickled an octopus from the rocks. "They have
the intelligence of a three-year-old child." Slotted
eyes measured me. Look, fear. Once an hour they jetted

across the tank till they weakened and died. Floodlights
useless in the ink and harbour water icy down my spine.
All autumn I grew in skill and grace, herding the old
sturgeon from the shadows of the back tank into

the limelight. Sea cucumber, anemone, sea feather.
Between shows I finned backstage to clean the glass,
watching the tourists on the other side watching me,
then swam into the dark passage between tanks with

a hard on. There in the dark. There. In the dark
I back-flipped, hung upside-down, busted up
shoals of sunfish, jack-knifed and sank
to the sand, where rock crab performed pliés.

Keeping watch

When the sun hauls down, a friend shows me the entrails
of a dog. "What does this mean?" he wants to know.

I'm thinking of the girl in the teal dress and no underwear
that I see in the city, and of the bluetick hound Emmett

that I returned to the pound because he howled and shit
in the house and otherwise ran wild. "An uncertain future,"

I tell my friend, "is where we're headed, no doubt. There's
a shooting star to prove it. There's another for good measure."

I wake with a sob at midnight, no stars, no good plan, alone.
Who can figure the entrails of a dog into something useful?

I kissed Lorraine by a clipped forest–stumps weathered silver–
while men fished from a pier and traffic roared, and my stomach

rose against my heart, the same way Emmett rose against
everything that wanted to keep him still. I want to be wise

enough to die rehearsed, but not before I make peace with
those I've wronged. Let them come singly and test the strength

of my resolve. I won't sleep. The bole of the tree is too rough.
Lorraine's brown eyes keep watch. O she's someone to tell

how brave I am, her skin so soft. But I do sleep well.
I wake with dew on my hair, the field silent. In the mist

two children hold hands while an untethered horse grazes and
the sky changes. Pale thighs under a green dress. On the horizon

my father has begun to plough. My beautiful mother.
An overgrown track through dense green sunshine.

Acknowledgments

Thanks to Ashlan Grey for accepting me into his life; David Roomy for arranging the meeting between the writer and the therapist; my sister Julie for her adventurer's heart; Marnie Parsons for seeing this book into print and being exactly where she should be; Patricia Young for her friendship and invaluable editorial help.

Deep gratitude for the many years of love to Marlene Cookshaw.

Thanks to the Canada Council for its very significant support during the writing of these poems.

Some of the poems appeared in magazines. "This longing," "Angels" and "Ferry" in *Fiddlehead*; "Hope Bay," "Well/Spring" and "Now that we are" in *Event*; "Heart room" and "Prison life" in *Prism international*; "At the rubbish heap" and "Shortcut" in *Grain*; "After the duel," "Another Sistine Chapel" and "Cabin" in *Prairie Fire*; "The Sutler" in *Arc*; and a selection of the Samurai poems in *The Malahat Review*.

Michael Kenyon was born in Sale, England, but has lived most of his life on the west coast of Canada. He is the author of seven books of fiction and poetry; his work has appeared in a number of anthologies and magazines, and has aired on CBC. For many years he served on the editorial board of *The Malahat Review*. He now works as a free-lance editor, and has a therapy practice in process-oriented psychology and jin shin do® bodymind acupressure on Pender Island and in Vancouver.